# THE EFFECTIVE BUSINESS PLAN

Michael Lane

Easyway Guides

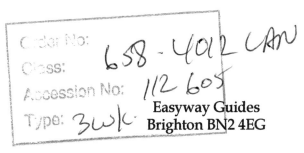
Easyway Guides
Brighton BN2 4EG

© Straightforward Publishing

ISBN 1900694 88 3

Printed by CATS Solutions Swindon Wiltshire.

Cover design by Straightforward Graphics.

The information in this book is correct at the time of going
to press. The author and publisher have no liability for
errors or omissions contained within or for any changes in
the law since publication.

# THE EFFECTIVE BUSINESS PLAN

## CONTENTS

7

# INTRODUCTION

The latest in the series of publications in the Straightforward Guides series, The Straightforward Business Plan aims to give the reader a clear and concise introduction to the various aspects of effective business planning.

This book has been produced with a view to providing the reader with a practical understanding of what is involved in the process of business planning. As such, it is targeted at those individuals and organizations who have no experience of business planning but would benefit from an understanding of these processes.

Organizations which will benefit include; sole traders, partnerships, small companies and voluntary organizations on the one hand, and students of business studies and economics on the other. The book also aims to provide a comprehensive insight into business planning for anyone hoping to start up their own business.

The book includes invaluable information on setting up a business, employment law, marketing and also finance. A model business plan is included which will help in the initial stages of business growth.

The whole process of business planning involves thinking and asking questions, and it is to these questions we now turn. Although most people who are faced with the prospect of producing a business plan, in particular in response to a request from their bank manager, feel daunted, the process is actually straightforward and with the aid of this book the task should be that much simpler.

# THE BUSINESS PLAN

# 1

# THE BUSINESS PLAN

## What is a business plan?

When answering this question, it is tempting to say that a business plan is a document which the budding entrepreneur can present to his or her bank manager as a means of assuring the latter of the viability of the proposed business, thereby securing start up funding.

In a sense, this is true. Increasingly, banks are refusing to finance small businesses, simply because so many have gone bust over the last ten years. Moreover, they have done so, according to many economic commentators, precisely because such small businesses have not thought about how it is they are going to survive and prosper in what is almost always a very competitive environment; they have not produced a business plan.

It is, therefore, erroneous to see business plan as simply a tool for negotiation with the bank manager. A business plan is, above all, a strategic document which assists the entrepreneur to think very carefully about all the aspects of the business that they are getting involved in. A good business plan will illustrate detailed research and evidence around such aspects of business as:

- the product/service; what exactly is it? It may be obvious to you, but unless you spell it out it may not be clear to your customers;

- the market; is there evidence of demand for your goods and services? Is the competition fierce? Are you entering a niche market? Is the market prone to fluctuation for any reason? If so, how do you propose to deal with this?

- your unique selling point (usp); what is it that makes your goods and services better than those of your competitors? Price? Quality? Anything else?

- yourself; have you got what it takes to be successful in your line of business? What relevant experience/training have you had? How do you propose to remedy any shortcomings in these respects?

- business development; what sort of life span are you putting on the business? What are your ultimate business objectives? Growth? Diversification?

- capital funding; what level of funding, if any, do you need to start up your own business? How much money can you afford to put into it?

- management and personnel; are you intending to employ other people? If so, what will their roles be? How will they relate to you? Are you aware of the legal and cost implications of employing staff.

- legal requirements; is your proposed business subject to certain legal requirements, eg, health and safety legislation, fire regulations, VAT, licensing etc.

- location and premises; from where do you propose

to run your business? Does location matter? What size of premises do you need and what do they cost? Is it feasible and/or desirable to work from home?

- budgeting; what are your overheads and likely level of income? Is there any scope for price variation in order to cope with increased competition?

- cash flow; at what points in the year will you face big bills? When can you expect an upturn in sales? What level of overdraft, if any, will you need to service the business?

These are the key questions which any good business plan will address, and it is the process of answering them-and thinking about them-which is most beneficial to the entrepreneur.

**How long must a business plan be?**

There are no golden rules regarding the length of a business plan. Always, the most important aspect of the plan is the quality of research, evidence and information provided. Needless to say, however, if a business plan purports to cover a long period of time, 10,20, 30 years for example-it will inevitably entail the provision of more information, thus elongating the size of the document.

Large businesses sometimes have business plans which cover a period of up to 30 years. Small businesses, if they have a business plan, normally cover a period of 2-3 years. In the case of new businesses, it is sometimes a good idea to have a business plan for the first year of trading only, to "test the water" and to review the plan at the end of the first year, producing what might be a more realistic 2-3 year plan, based on the experiences of the first year. As a rule of thumb, however, a business plan should aim to be around 10-12 sides of paper in length, with relevant appendices attached (cash flow forecast, profit and loss forecast, budget calculations etc)

## What resources do you need to produce a business plan?

Large companies producing 20-30 year business plans employ highly qualified accountants and financial experts with highly sophisticated computer equipment to assist them in the drafting of their business plans. As a consequence, the small independent trader may feel somewhat ill qualified to produce such a plan. However, it is possible to produce a business plan without expensive equipment and expert advice. In particular, because the proposed business is small there are less complications which experts would normally deal with. A business plan can be produced by a small trader if he/she has the following resources and assets:

- time

- commitment

- numeracy

- literacy

- patience

These are all the human resources required to produce a business plan. The only other things needed are a pen and piece of paper!

Now read the key points from Chapter 1.

## Key Points from Chapter 1

- A Business plan is a strategic document which assists the business person to think very clearly and carefully about all aspects of the business they are involved in, or getting involved in.

- A good business plan will illustrate detailed research and evidence around all aspects of business.

- A good business plan will help you to understand your unique selling point as a business.

- There are no golden rules regarding the length of a business plan.

- A business plan can be produced by anyone with basic resources.

# THE BUSINESS

# 2

# THE BUSINESS

When putting pen to paper to draw up your business plan, three fundamental questions need to be addressed:

- What is the nature of the business that you are entering into?

- What is it about you that makes you a competent business person a) generally and b) in relation to your particular business?

  - What is it that makes your particular product or service special? What is your unique selling point (usp)?

**Business description-service and product**
At first, describing your business plan in detail might seem like entering into irrelevant detail, after all, a butchers a butcher and an architects an architect... or are they? Take the butcher. The butcher could have anyone of a number of usp's, including the following:

- specialist in continental meats and sausages

- catering for certain ethnic/religious groups (halal, kosher)

- provider of non factory farmed products
- provider of certain ready made dishes, eg, specially marinaded chops for barbecues, skewer kebabs etc

- provider of home delivery service

- employment of highly trained, qualified staff, able to give advice on both products and food preparation.

- lower cost than competitors

- provision of delicatessen services

- particularly convenient location

It is important to consider very carefully about what exactly it is you are proposing to sell because in so doing you are forced to think about your "competitive edge", your USP. The consequence of not having a competitive edge is, quite simply, failure. If it is not failure, then it means that you are operating a monopoly, or entering into a market in which demand outstrips supply. Even then, it is crucial to remember that the market or excess demand should not last forever.

Let us think about an architect. An architect's unique selling point could be that he or she:

- is particularly highly qualified or experienced in their job, with     an excellent track record and a long list of clients

- specialises in certain types of design, eg, adapted rooms for people with disabilities

- caters for a particular client or set of clients, eg, public sector landlords

- provides other, related services (eg surveying, quantity surveying etc)

Consequently, in describing your business you inevitably have to address the issue of USP.

**Exercise 1**
Draw up a list of possible unique selling points for the following businesses:

-a bookshop
-a clothes manufacturer
-a cinema
-a solicitors practice
-a public house

**You as a business person**

Have you got what it takes to be a successful business manager? Do you have the necessary skills, qualifications and experience to enable you to be successful in the field of business that you have chosen? Any good business plan will contain within it a C.V of all of the key staff involved in the business. Unsurprisingly, it will contain a particularly detailed CV of the person-or persons-responsible for running the business, the managers.

At this point, it is important to bear in mind the fact that the business plan can be, and usually is, a marketing document-that is, a document that will be read by possible funders and, in some cases, clients. Therefore, exactly how you word and present the CV needs to be taken into consideration.

In respect of employed staff, a paragraph outlining their relevant qualifications, skills and experience should suffice for any reader of the business plan. For the owners and managers, more detail should be entered into.

The CV should include certain personal details relating to the managers or owners (if different) of the business, including name, address and date of birth. The reasons for giving name and address are obvious; no one is going to want to do business with an anonymous client. Date of birth is usually something that may not be of interest to some readers of the business plan. However, a bank manager would want to know if it was viable to lend money to someone whose age suggests that they might not be in business long enough to pay back any loan that they take out, or whether the owner of the business is likely to be sufficiently mature as to handle well the responsibilities of a business person.

The above information constitutes formal detail, and it should come at the start of the business plan, preceding the business description. It is in describing the skills, qualifications and experience of the staff, especially the owners and managers, that the business plan explains how the proposed business is to be viable in terms of

personnel.
What are the particular skills, qualifications and experience that are required to run any business successfully? A successful business person will have skills/qualifications/experience in relation to all of the following, albeit in varying proportions:

- personnel management (especially important if employing staff)

- financial management

- initiative, dynamism, imagination

- leadership

- social skills

If the CV's of the manager in the business plan successfully demonstrate the above, then the business plan goes a long way towards convincing the reader that the author of the plan is a serious business-person.
If employing staff, the author of the plan should highlight any experience that they have had in supervising staff. Such experience might have been gained in previous employment, eg, as a shop manager. Alternatively, it may have been gained in a voluntary capacity (eg, as a management committee member of a local charity).

It might also be demonstrated by reference to relevant professional qualifications. In addition, if the author cannot legitimately refer to any of the above, he or she can draw upon comparable experience of supervising people in a formal capacity, perhaps as a teacher or nursery nurse. Finally, if this is not too feasible then it is possible to demonstrate personnel management by reference to informal experience of supervising people.

Similar to the above, there are numerous ways of demonstrating financial management skills. For example, it is possible to point to previous employment experience as an accountant, a bookkeeper etc. On the other hand, you may have a professional qualification in finance or you may have gained experience in a voluntary capacity. Lastly, you can always draw upon your informal experience of budget management, either through the family or some other capacity.

Having considered your business and the skills and talents of those people who will run it, it is necessary to take the next step in the formulation of the plan, that is the consideration of the structure of your business. There are a number of ways of setting up your business, from sole trader to partnership to limited company. It is vital that you understand the various structures that your business can operate within and that you have chosen the right one.

Now read the key points from Chapter 2

## Key points from Chapter 2

- There are three fundamental questions to be addressed when putting together a business plan: What is the nature of the business that you are entering into? What is it about you that makes you a competent business person? What is it that makes your particular product or service special? What is your unique selling point?

- It is vital to understand the various structures that your business can operate within.

# STRUCTURE OF THE BUSINESS

# 3

# THE STRUCTURE OF YOUR BUSINESS

There are various structures within which your business can operate and it is essential, when formulating your business plan that you understand the nature of each structure.

**The sole or proprietary business**

This is a business owned by one person. If you are operating alone then this may be suitable for your purposes. The person and the business are legally one and the same. It does not matter what or who you trade as the business is inseparable from yourself, as opposed to a limited company, which is a separate entity.

All financial risk is taken by that one person and all that persons assets are included in that risk. The one big advantage is that all decisions can be taken by the one person without interference.

A second advantage is that the administrative costs of running a sole business are small, if your business is VAT registered then you will need to keep records, as you will for the inland revenue. However, there are no other legal requirements.

## Partnerships

A partnership is a business where two or more people are joined by an agreement to run that business together. The agreement is usually written, given the potential pitfalls that can arise from a partnership.

Liabilities which may arise are shared jointly and severally and this should be made clear to anyone entering a partnership. Even if you only have 1% of the business you will still be responsible for 100% of the liability. All personal assets of each partner are at risk if the business fails.

Decisions are taken jointly, as laid down by the partnership agreement. If the agreement lays down that partners have differing decision making capacity dependent upon their shareholding then it could be that, in a three way partnership, the decision making process may be hampered because a decision cannot be reached unless the major investor is present.

It is very important indeed to consider the nature of the agreement that you are entering into and it may also be advisable to take legal advice.

Partnership usually reflects the way that business was capitalised although other factors may be taken into consideration. For example, an expert in a particular field may join with an investor to create a 50/50 partnership.

It is very advisable indeed to consider carefully the ramifications of entering into a partnership. Many such arrangements end in tears, with both partners hostile to each other. Personal bankruptcy can occur as can the ruin of the partner(s).

Profits are usually shared between partners in accordance with the terms in the agreement.

**The limited liability company**

This type of company has evolved over the years and provides a framework within which a business can operate effectively. A limited company is usually the best vehicle for business, in all but the smallest of business. It is certainly the only sensible answer if capital is being introduced by those who are not actively involved in running the business (shareholders).

Shareholders inject capital and receive a return (dividend) in proportion to the capital they invest. They are eligible to attend an annual general meeting to approve or otherwise the way the directors are running the business. Annual General meetings also determine how much of the profit will be distributed to shareholders.

Voting is in accordance with the number of shares held and the meeting can replace all or any of the directors if a majority are dissatisfied with them.

Shareholders can, if a majority request, call an Extraordinary General meeting To question directors about performance, outside the Cycle of Annual General Meetings.

Control of the company is in the hands of directors who are appointed by the shareholders to run the company on their behalf.

The company is a legal entity in its own right and stands alone from the directors and shareholders, who have limited liability.

When a company is created it will have an Authorised Shareholding" That specifies the limit of a shareholders liability. If all shares have been issued then shareholders are not liable for any more debts that the company may accrue.

**The franchise**

Franchising is just one word to describe a number of varying business relationships-some big, some small, some complex. Essentially, a properly constructed franchise involves a well established company offering an individual the opportunity to trade under its corporate name. The company will also provide well proven know how, a marketing programme, training, research and development facilities and, often, bulk buying and administrative facilities.

The individual, in return, pays for the privilege-usually by way of an initial fee, followed by a continuing levy, most often expressed as a percentage of sales.

The British Franchise Association, 75A Bell Street, Henley on Thames, Oxfordshire RG9 2BD will advise you on the various pitfalls and can point you in the right direction. From them, you can purchase a "Franchisee pack" which contains some useful hints on being a franchisee and also includes an up to date list of those companies which are members of the Association.

It is essential, when considering forming a company, that you have a clear idea of what type of structure should relate to your business. If you need further advice concerning business structure, you should contact the Department of Trade and Industry, whose address is at the rear of this book.

## Patents and registered designs

In order to grow, industry must continually create and develop new ideas. Innovation is expensive and innovators need protection, to ensure that others cannot pirate their ideas. All of the above items are known as "intellectual property" and, with the exception of copyright, in order to register and protect your intellectual property, you need to contact the patent office. Their address can be obtained from the Chartered Institute of Patent Agents, whose number is at the rear of this book.

## Patent

If you or your company have produced what you consider is a unique product or process, it is very important to register it as soon as possible, before disclosing it to anyone. The granting of a patent gives the patentee a monopoly to make, use or sell an invention for a fixed period of time. This is currently a maximum of twenty years.

## Registered designs

This involves registering what you consider to be a new design. The proprietor must register before offering for sale in the U.K the new design.

## Trademarks

A trademark is a means of identification-whether a word or a logo-which is used in the course of trade in order to identify and distinguish to the purchaser that the goods in question are yours. A good trademark is a very important marketing aid and you are strongly advised to register it.

## Service marks

This register extends the trademark to cover not only goods but also services. If you are running a hotel for example, you can now register your service mark if you have one.

## Copyright

Unlike the other four categories, copyright is established by evidence of creation, and protection is automatic. To safeguard your position, it might be sensible to deposit your work with your bank or your solicitor or send a copy of your work to yourself by registered post.

It should be noted that there is no copyright attached to a name or title, only the work itself.

Having given thought to the likely structure of your business, we need now to consider, in chapter four, the right location for your business and also questions relating to the employment and management of staff.

Now read the key points from Chapter 3

Key points from Chapter 3

• There are a number of structures within which your business can operate and it is vital that you find the correct one for you.

• You can operate as a sole trader, partnership, limited company, or franchise.

• You should consider areas of patent and copyright that may affect your business.

# LOCATION OF THE BUSINESS

# 4

# LOCATION AND PREMISES-MAKING THE RIGHT CHOICE

## Location of your business

To be within easy reach of your customers may be vital or it may be totally unimportant. If you have a retail business, location is a major consideration. If you are in mail order, you can operate from anywhere in the country so far as your customers are concerned. If you are a wholesaler, do you require a showroom? If you are operating a factory, do you anticipate the requirement for a factory shop? is it simply a question of being conveniently located for your customers or are you relying on passing trade? It is vital that, in assessing the right location, you first clearly define the extent to which you need to make yourself accessible to your customers.

In an ideal world, you should be looking to acquire the right accommodation for your scale of operation today and for your expansion plans this year, next year and some years in the future. This applies whether you are looking for a shop, an office, a workshop or a factory unit. Before you start looking for new premises, work out carefully just what it is you need now.

## The important questions to consider are:

- How many square feet of offices/storage space/workshop/showroom?

- How many square feet of employees facilities?

- How much car parking space?

- How much outside storage for deliveries, storage and packing?

If you are uncertain as to what precisely you need, or you feel that the shape of your business is going to alter substantially and in the short term, do not commit yourself to a hefty purchase, or even as much as a five year lease. Go instead for a temporary solution, while you determine what your long-term requirements are likely to be.

Never enter into a lengthy commitment unless you feel that the premises are likely to suit you in the long term. Whether you are buying a freehold or acquiring a lease, take independent professional advice on the value. Hire a surveyor who will tell you whether the asking price or rent is fair. Whatever your business, the cost of your premises is going to represent a major overhead. If you get it wrong, you will go out of business.

It is essential to establish that not only can the property be used for the purpose for which we want it, but also that the planning consent will cover any future business development.

## Working from home

Particularly if you are starting a new business, the idea of working from home is attractive. It enables you to keep your overheads to a minimum, allows you to work the long hours necessary in the establishment of a business, and leaves your options open-if the business does not work out, you are not committed to an industrial property. It needs to be recognized, however, that working from home can cause considerable problems.

Strictly speaking, if you plan to run a business from home, almost certainly you will need approval or permission either from someone or some authority. There are two kinds of restrictions which may affect your ability to run your business from home. The first is a series of contractual relationships which you may have already entered into, such as a tenancy or lease. The second is that imposed by local authorities-planning, highways, health and safety.

## Planning permission

If you want to make a significant alteration to your house in order to accommodate your business, you will need planning permission or building regulations approval. This includes building an extension, loft conversion, in fact almost anything except extremely simple alterations

## Change of use

Local authorities state that consent has to be sought for

any change of use. The interpretation of change of use is difficult but what you have to decide is whether what you wish to do constitutes a genuine material change of use of the building.

You should make sure that you have insurance to cover your business activity within your home. If you have an accident which occurs as a direct result of your business then your insurance will not cover it.

## Health and Safety at work

Whatever your position in relationship to your premises, i.e., leasehold or freehold, under the terms of the Health and Safety at Work Act You have certain obligations to protect yourself, your staff, your customers and your suppliers. Health and Safety Legislation is very important and attention should be paid to it.

## Inspectors

There are two types of inspector-local authority inspectors and fire authority inspectors. Local Authority inspectors are concerned with premises where the main activities are:

- The sale or storage of goods for retail or wholesale distribution.

- Office activities

- Catering Services

- Provision of residential accommodation

- Consumer services provided in shop premises

- Dry Cleaning in coin operated units in launderettes

- The keeping of wild animals for exhibition to the public

- Fire Authority inspectors

The fire authority requires that a place of work should have a fire certificate, and in order for your business to get a fire certificate, the premises need to be inspected. The fire authority will wish to see that there is adequate provision for a means of escape in case of fire, and the necessary amount of equipment. The Fire inspectors will advise you these facilities are inadequate, tell you how they can be put right and then re-inspect the premises when you have carried out the necessary work.

Now read the key points from chapter 4.

Key points from Chapter 4

• Location of your business may be important depending on the nature of the business.

• When considering premises size and space are key considerations, as is car parking.

Depending on your business, it may be possible to work from home.

# EMPLOYING PEOPLE

# 5

# EMPLOYING PEOPLE

At first you may be able to run your business by yourself or with help from your family. But if not, as your business expands, you may need to employ people. Before doing this, some businesses may consider it worthwhile subcontracting work. This may be more cost effective in ironing out short term trading highs and lows. However, if you do need to take on employees, then you must do certain things.

**What are my responsibilities as an employer?**

You must give every employee a written statement of terms of employment. At the time of publication, by law, all employees working 16 or more hours a week must be given a written statement of terms after they have worked 13 weeks in the job.

This statement must include the following:
- name of employer

- name of employee, job title and description

- hours of work

- pay details, including how often the employee is paid
- holidays

- grievance procedures

- sickness and injury procedures

- pension schemes

- length of notice needed to end employment

- disciplinary rules, including dress and behaviour

**National Insurance Contributions**

If you employ anybody, either full time or part time, you must take tax and national insurance contributions (NIC's) from their wages, and you must also pay the employers share of the NIC's, always consult your local contributions agency office. There are different tax and National Insurance Rules depending on your circumstances.

**Discrimination and the law**

It is against the law for an employer or a would-be employer to advertise a job that in anyway discriminates against race or sex. After taking on an employee, the anti discrimination laws still apply to all other parts of the employees job, including wages and holidays.

**Health and safety**

Make sure you are in line with the health and safety regulations which lay down minimum standards for fire precautions and other safety issues. Contact your local health and safety executive for advice and information which will help you to set up and maintain safe and legal working conditions for employees.

## Trade Unions

Make sure that you know about the various laws which safeguard your employees rights to choose whether to join a trade union.

## Tax and National Insurance-more details

Once you regularly employ people, you are responsible for deducting their income tax and National Insurance Contributions, and paying your own employers NI contributions. When you take on someone, you need to tell your local tax office. You will be sent documents which will show you how much you need to take out of each employees wages, and where to send the money. You must record each employees earnings and tax and National Insurance Contributions, and tell your local tax office about these amounts each year.

In the case of national Insurance, The contributions for your employees will be in two parts. You must pay one part and your employee will pay the other. These contributions depend on how much you pay your employee. The Inland Revenue will collect them at the same time as they collect any tax. Your local contributions agency office will be able to give you more advice on National Insurance.

Your personal insurance depends on your circumstances. If you are a company director, you will be treated in a similar way to your employees. You will be classed as an employee of your company and will pay contributions in the same way as your employees. But, there is no special way to assess directors National Insurance. You should contact the Contributions Agency Office for advice on this matter. If you are a sole trader, or partner, your contributions will be charged at the same rate each week. You must pay them every month by direct debit or every three months when you receive a bill. You may also have to pay an extra contribution for any profits your company makes. This is assessed and collected along with Income tax. You should tell the contribution's agency office as soon as you become self- employed.

**The law and you as an employer**

Having considered some of the main issues involved in employing people, you may want to become more acquainted with the following issues and how the law deals with them:

- terms of employment

- redundancy

- insolvency

- pregnancy

- suspension on medical grounds

- sick leave

- health and safety
- union membership
- itemised pay statements
- continuous employment
- time off for public duties
- unfair dismissal
- rights on ending employment
- union secret ballots
- limit on payment
- race discrimination
- sex discrimination
- equal pay
- disabled workers
- picketing

Although all of the above areas may not affect you, particularly in the early stages of development, if you do intend to employ staff then you should at least acquaint yourself with the areas.

## Recruiting and motivating employees-Doing it yourself

You can do your own recruiting by advertising locally or in special; papers. Or you could write to colleges and schools for candidates.

## Job centres and employment agencies

The Job Centre, the Job Club, or the local careers office are all in business to fit people to jobs. Job Centres or careers offices give their services for free, but an employment agency could cost you as much as 20% of

the employees first years salary.
## Training

Training is necessary to make sure that staff know why
and how a job has to be done. It can also help make
them more efficient and help increase their productivity.
Investing wisely in staff training pays off in the long
run.

## The personal approach

The better you treat your employees, the better they will
treat you. If you are well mannered, punctual and
committed they will be too. Show them that they are
valued, encourage their interest in the business and ask
them for suggestions. They will probably respond
positively but don't be patronising.

Have confidence in your workforce and allow them to
get on with the job. Checking everything they do creates
resentment and not much else. All good managers are
able to delegate. Good delegation is really what
management is all about. You could also set targets and
give bonuses. This way, you will encourage your
employees to work harder. As a result you will increase
productivity and waste less time. Payment-you must
always pay wages on time and at competitive rates.
Show appreciation-praise for a job well done is a real
incentive. But try not to be over friendly. This is difficult
when you are working one to one, but it might reduce
your authority and it will be difficult to take a firm line
if you ever need to.

Now read the key points from Chapter 5

Key points from chapter 5

- When employing people you will need to be familiar with employment law and also the structure of the various government agencies that exist to help the would be employer.

# MARKETING OF A BUSINESS

# 6

# MARKETING

The next step in formulating our business plan is to look at sales, which in turn means looking at the market and considering the most appropriate form of market research. Sales are vital to any business. Whatever you produce, you must be able to sell. This is necessary in order to survive.

You must be satisfied that there is a demand for your proposed business and you must be able to determine how you can investigate the market in which you want to operate, how many potential clients there are in either the catchment area you operate in or the wider area. If you work in publishing for example then clearly the market for your product would be different for that of a baker or butcher or plumber. A lot of thought needs to be given to this area.

## Market Research

The tool that is used to determine demand for a product is market research. Market research can be cheap and simple or highly complex depending on how you approach it and what you might want to find out.

Market research, or effective market research should be able to provide you with information as to what people want and also how much they want and what they will pay for it. Competition which might exist should also come to light.

You should not be put off by competition nor should you believe that because there appears to be no local supplier that what you produce will sell. No supplier may mean no demand and competition may mean established demand.

The concept behind all market research is simple-the practice is often not and unless you have a lot of money the costs may be prohibitive. A good example might be a supermarket.

A potential supermarket would want to know concrete facts in order to establish demand. For example, in terms of the percentage of the population, the average number of visits made to a supermarket each year. This they may well be able to establish from their own records if they are part of a chain.

Secondly they would want to know, what distance people are prepared to travel in order to visit a supermarket. This will vary a lot but they would be interested in establishing a national average.

With these two facts the supermarket can then establish the catchment area population for the proposed supermarket. Now they need to know something about the competition. How many supermarkets are there in the catchment zone which might have an effect on the proposed supermarket? This is easily established. However, more difficult to determine is the effect on your potential business. If we suppose that the supermarket decides that only 30% of the catchment area is exposed to competition and that they expect that 50% of that 30% would continue to use the supermarkets they presently use. This means an adjustment to predicted customer base.

However, competition comes from other shops not just supermarkets This is why calculations are based on average figures since this additional competition will be fairly standard throughout the country. A survey will be carried out in the locality to check that there are no special factors to consider-special factors which may cause adjustments to the predicted customer base either way.

The next question to be considered is; what is the average spend per visit per customer? Supermarkets will almost certainly be able to answer that one from existing records.

From this data, they can predict gross sales and so the net operating profit. If this is not high enough to justify the expenditure, they might be reluctant to proceed with siting a supermarket.

The above is a simple model and does not take into account a number of complications but it does give an idea of how market research is carried out. There are two very important factors to be considered-average conditions in the industry and catchment area population, or a knowledge of that population. Although the example given covers selling to the general public the same principle applies when considering selling to other business.

It may be possible to determine industry averages by approaching trade associations. A visit to the bank is also very worthwhile as most high street banks keep statistics which they would be willing to make available. A further source of statistics might be a major supplier in an industry.

Somewhat easier is to determine the magnitude of the target market. Businesses generally fall into one or two categories: those where the customer comes to the business to place the order and those where the business goes to the customer to get the order.

In the first category, the size of your target market will be a percentage of the local population. The size of the population can be found by contacting the records office at your local authority. The percentage which applies to your proposed business will be far harder to determine. The classic method is simple-ask a large enough sample to provide an accurate picture. This is easier said than done. A great deal of research experience is necessary in order to be able to design a questionnaire which can elicit all the right information.

If you can afford it, you could consider employing a market research agency to assist you. If you cannot afford it then you should spend time considering exactly what you want to ask and what you are trying to establish. There are many other places which will hold the sort of information you might need. Your local training enterprise agency (TEC) or the trade association relevant to your business will be only too pleased to assist you.

Once you have established your target market, you might wish to consider exactly how you sell to that market. Easy if you have a shop in the middle of a busy shopping area, at least easier than if you produce books and have to cast your net far wider. It might be useful at this stage to look at marketing in a little more depth.

## Marketing

You have carried out some form of research and now you are in a position where you wish to bring to peoples attention your product. Obviously different media are more suited to some businesses than others.

Marketing covers a whole range of activities designed to "identify, anticipate, and satisfy customer needs at a profit" (Chartered Institute of Marketing).

**Three questions need to be looked at:**

• When do customers want needs satisfied

• How do the customers want the need fulfilled

• How much are the customers prepared to pay for that fulfilment

Having found the answers to those questions we have to decide how best to communicate to the target market our ability to meet their needs at a price that they can afford-and communicate that ability to them at a price that we can afford.

TOWER HAMLETS COLLEGE
Learning Centre
Poplar High Street
LONDON
E14 0AF

There are various options that we can consider. However, some of these options are expensive and may well not be within our reach.

## Advertising

Advertising takes various forms. It is exceedingly difficult, unless you have deep pockets, to try to deduce the real effectiveness of whichever form of advertising you decide to employ. For example, is it cost effective to spend £800 on a small advert in a tabloid for one day if that £800 could be spent on something longer lasting.

Advertising hoardings and posters are one way. These tend to cover not only billboards but also tubes trains and buses. Hoardings are seen repeatedly by a wide and ever changing audience in the locality of your choice. They are usually inexpensive.

## Leaflets

Leaflets can be distributed on a door to door basis (either to other businesses or to individual residences) or they can be given to individuals in the street. However, leaflets can also be thrown away as many see them as junk mail. The result is that leaflets tend to have a low strike rate. Leaflets can also be delivered as inserts in magazines and newspapers. Magazines direct leaflets to specific audiences and newspapers to local areas. Both can prove expensive and again will be discarded more often than not.

A more effective use of leaflets is to have them available in places where the target market will see them. The classic case here is for businesses offering non residential facilities for holidaymakers. These can usually be found in hotels and guesthouses.

Another use of the leaflet is that of a poster in a newsagent or on other notice boards. This can be effective when being used to attract a defined group of the population who gather together in one place where leaflets cannot be made available. Universities or schools might be a good example.

## Directories

Directories will fall into two categories-local and trade. Local directories such as yellow pages are well known mediums of advertising and they are reasonably priced, sometimes free. However, the effectiveness of such advertising depends on what you are doing and also where the ad is placed. Some businesses tend towards directories such as Thompson's because they have less advertisers and are cheaper.

Trade directories are different by their nature. They are unlikely to benefit new businesses as they can be expensive and are in some cases, nationally distributed.

This is of little use if your business is local, of more use if your product is distributed nationally. There are now a number of local area and regional directories, often produced by trade associations. Some are available as a book or on disc for use with computers. Those who subscribe to the disc system often receive monthly or quarterly updates.

## Advertising in magazines

Magazines fall into three categories-general national, local or specialist. Magazines tend to be more expensive to advertise ion than newspapers but can be more effective. Magazines have a longer life expectancy than newspapers and are often passed on to other readers. Specialist magazines are read by specific people who may form part of your desired target audiences. It is worthwhile bearing in mind that most magazine are national.

## Newspaper advertising

National newspapers can obviously reach a lot of people but also tend to be expensive. They are also of little value to those offering local services. Local newspaper advertising can be more effective and also cheaper. Free newspapers are cheaper but can be less effective as they also tend to be seen as junk mail.

## Television advertising

It is highly unlikely that television advertising will be relevant in the early years of a business. To launch a television advertising campaign is very expensive indeed. Therefore, this medium will only be a consideration later on, if at all.

## Radio advertising

This form of advertising would only be effective if there are sufficient numbers of listeners in the target market. However, in the right circumstances it can be useful and relatively inexpensive. Timing is very important in this medium as you need to target your slots at the most appropriate times and on the most appropriate programme for your intended target audience.

## Using an advertising agent

Whether or not an advertising agency is employed will be a matter for the individual business concerned. This decision is down to cost. All businesses placing advertising should set an advertising budget. It could be that placing part of your budget with an agent proves far more cost effective than designing your own campaign. Agents are usually good at designing and placing adverts and can negotiate discounts with various media. It is certainly worthwhile consulting an agent in order to get an idea of what they can do for you, at the same time raising your own awareness of the direction you should be taking.

## Direct mail

Direct mail falls into two categories: untargeted or blanket mailing or targeted. Targeted mail is usually far more effective as untargeted mail can be very expensive and also wasteful. Existing customers of a business are well defined and easily targeted. The secret with direct mail is to keep it short, simple and do it as often as is necessary.

## Using sales representatives or agents

Whether or not you choose to use representatives or agents will depend on a number of factors. Where there are few sales required and the selling of a good is complex there may be the need for a representative. Where the product is simple and can be described in an advertisement or leaflet it is unlikely to be necessary to use a representative. There are two main types of representation, the representative or agent.

The representative is a paid member of staff who may or may not receive a bonus or commission based on results. All the representatives running costs will be borne by the business. An agent is a freelance who meets his or her own costs and is paid only on results.

The advantage of using the representative is that he or she uses their entire time devoted to your business and is under your total control.

The agent costs little to run. However, he or she is not totally dedicated to your business. If other products are easier to sell he may ignore yours altogether.

As you can see, there are a number of ways to reach your target audience, once that target audience has been defined. A lot of thought needs to be given to market research and marketing. All too often, they are the first areas to go through the window in search of savings or simply because you are too busy.

However, well-defined marketing can produce corresponding increase in profits and a clear strategy is an essential part of any business plan.

## Pricing Your Product

A well thought out pricing plan is essential to the future prosperity of your business, and will also help you to make the most of your opportunities.

To develop the right pricing plan for your business, you need to start by working out what your costs are. You need to look at what your competitors are charging and try to estimate what your service or product is worth to your customers.

By knowing what costs you are incurring, you will be able to work out what your "break even" point is. How much do you need to sell before your business covers all its costs, including your own (essential) drawings, but before it makes a profit. Unless you can identify what your break-even point is, you could operate at a loss, without realising until it is too late.

### Your Costs

Costs can be divided into fixed (overheads) and variable (direct) costs. Fixed costs include your essential personal expenses, such as Mortgage, food etc, as well as rent, heating and lighting wages and interest charges. They tend to stay the same no matter how much you sell. Variable costs, however, increase or decrease according to your level of sales.

The most obvious cost here is the actual cost of materials required to manufacture the product but can include other things such as transport, postage or additional labour. The price you charge for your product has to

71

cover all of the variable costs and contribute towards your overheads.

**Outlined below is an example of a break-even point.**

| Fred Peters Car Wash Ltd | Cost per Annum |
|---|---|
| Personal Drawings | 10,000 |
| National Insurance | 294 |
| Tax | 500 |
| Stationary | 100 |
| Advertising | 400 |
| Telephone | 320 |
| Depreciation of Van (over 5 years) | 1,000 |
| Petrol | 900 |
| Servicing | 300 |
| Road Tax Fund | 130 |
| Insurance | 320 |
| Business Insurance | 140 |
| Materials | 200 |
| Depreciation of Equipment | 200 |
| Bank Loan £3,000 @ 12% | 200 |

| | |
|---|---|
| Bank Charges | 100 |
| Accountants Fees | 300 |
| TOTAL | £15,404 |

Fred's essential personal drawings to cover his family expenses is £10,000. He operates a small car wash. He expects to work for 46 weeks a year, allowing for holidays, sickness etc. He estimates that he will work 38 hours per week.

*His annual output is therefore:*

46 weeks a year Times 38 hours times 0.5 cars per hour = 874

His break even point is

$$\frac{15,404}{874}$$

= £17.62 per car

After researching the market in his area, Fred believes he can confidently charge £20 per car, which will give him a reasonable profit.

## Competitors Prices

Unless your service or product is much better than others on the market, you would be unwise to charge a price which is too far above your competitors, as you will find sales very hard too achieve. On the other hand, a low price often implies low quality or low standards. Competing on price alone is a poor option. It is especially important for small businesses to differentiate themselves by other means, such as personal service, convenience or special skills.

Customers rarely buy on price alone and it is worth remembering that you can more easily reduce your prices than put them up.

If, when you work out what your prices should be, they do not cover your costs-look again at how you might make your business viable. For example, could you reduce any of your variable costs, could you get supplies more cheaply, can you negotiate a discount or find an alternative supplier? On your fixed costs, could you trim any other expenditure?

Think again about what you are offering. Could it be improved and sold at a higher price? Can you sell different products for more money to increase your profits? Would sales increase if you put up your prices and spent the extra income on advertising and promotion?

Every cost incurred in running your business must be recovered either by what you charge for your time, or by the amount you charge for your products. Profits will be made only after all of your costs have been covered. But you may decide to use different prices in different situations. For example, a plumber offering a 24 hour service might decide to charge a premium rate for his services if he is called out during the night to deal with an emergency, a different rate for weekends and another rate for normal working hours.

Achieving a range of prices for the variety of skills offered, taking into account the time you would be likely to spend on each job and the convenience factor your customers can give you the flexibility to stay competitive, yet still provide a satisfactory income.

Now read the key points from chapter 6

## Key Points from Chapter 6

- It is vital that you understand the market and the demand for your product.

- Effective market research, and an understanding of how this works, is vital to your business.

- Marketing covers a whole range of activities designed to identify, anticipate and satisfy customers at a profit.

- There are a number of ways of reaching customers to determine demand, advertising, leaflets, television, radio, direct mail and more. You may consider using an agent to help you.

- A well thought out pricing plan is vital to your business.

- Always take into account hidden costs when pricing goods.

# FINANCIAL CONTROL OF THE BUSINESS

# 7

# FINANCIAL CONTROL

In this chapter, we will consider the importance of financial control within the process of business planning. In particular, we will look at profit and loss forecasting, cashflow forecasting, effective book-keeping, tax and insurance and raising capital for your business.

## Profit and loss forecasting

A profit and loss forecast is a projection of what sales you think you will achieve, what costs you will incur in achieving those sales and what profit you will earn. There is a blank profit and loss forecast sheet in appendix to enable you to practice.

Having this information down on paper means that you will be able to refer to it, and adjust it as your business develops. Not all the headings will be relevant to you, so don't worry if you leave blank spaces.

There is an example of a profit and loss forecast overleaf which you can refer to.

## Cashflow forecast

A cashflow forecast, as the name suggests, forecasts the changes in the cash which comes into and out of your bank account each month. For example, your customers may pay you after one month, whereas you might pay out for rent or insurance in advance. At the same time, you will have to pay for certain costs such as materials or wages and will need to budget for this. There is a sample cashflow form in the appendix to enable you to practice.

## Preparing a Cashflow Forecast

Remember that a cashflow forecast helps you to evaluate the timing of money coming into and going out of your business. In showing you the "movement" of money it takes full account of the fact that you may often not be paid immediately for work done and, correspondingly, that you may not have to pay immediately for goods and services you acquire. An important purpose of a cashflow forecast is to reveal the gap between your cash receipts and payments. It will show you whether or not, for example, you might need to borrow, and if so, when you are most likely to require additional funds. It is very common for businesses to need more cash as they grow because of the difference in timing of receipts and payments.

## Other Terms

*Working Capital*
Working capital is the term often used to describe the short-term resources used by the business for everyday trading purposes. This consists of:

*Debtors*-these are customers you have sold to in credit, i.e., they owe you money.

*Creditors*-these are your suppliers who you have purchased from on credit, i.e., you owe them money.

*Stock*-this represents the value of materials you have purchased. They may be purchased for immediate resale or they may be in the process of being converted into a finished article.

*Cash*-this can either be the amount of physical cash you are holding or it may be money held in a current or bank deposit account.

All of the above have to be carefully controlled if your business is to prosper.

## Over-trading

A problem common to many small and growing businesses is what is described as "over trading". The more sales you make, the more money you will need to spend on funding material and debtors before you are paid for the sales. If your level of sales becomes too high and you do not have the necessary level of working capital to support it, you may simply run out of cash. This can be disastrous for your business and means that a full order book is not the only thing to strive for.

Even with a profitable business and a full order book, it is imperative to have enough cash available. Extra finance can help your cashflow and make it easier to avoid the pitfalls of over trading.

## Collecting money on time
For every day a customer delays payments, your profit

margin is eroded. You may have to pay interest charges on a loan or overdraft, when the money owed to you could be earning you interest instead.

### Check your customers ability to pay

Before you offer customers credit, check that they can meet their liabilities. You may want to take up bank references.

### Set out your terms of trading

Be specific about when you expect payment, for example, 30 days from the date of the invoice and make your customer aware in advance of work that you do.

### Set up a system

Set up a system which enables you to issue invoices promptly and shows you when invoices become overdue.

### Keep clear and accurate records

Inaccurate invoices or unclear records can be one of the main reasons for customers delaying payments. Make sure you send invoices punctually, to the right person at the right address.

### Collect your payment on time

Establish a collections routine and stick to it. Keep records of all correspondence and conversations. Give priority to your larger accounts, but chase smaller amounts too. If regular chasing does not produce results consider stopping further supplies to the customer. If payment is not obtained, don't hesitate to ask a reputable debt collection agency or solicitor to collect the money for you.

Your Business activities will consist of selling goods and/or services. At the same time you will have to spend money on behalf of the business, on the purchase or rent of premises, raw materials, equipment, stationery etc. etc. in order to conduct business.

Remember that every business transaction generates a financial transaction, all of which must be recorded in books of account on an on-going basis. It is a fundamental management requirement that this be done on a regular basis, at a minimum once a week. Leave it much longer, and sooner or later an iron law of accounting will come into operation. You will have mislaid a financial record or simply forgotten to request one or issue one. When you do get around to up-dating the books, they won' balance. Unless you can discover the error before the end of the financial year your accountant will be faced with the task of reconciling "incomplete records", which he or she will enjoy because of the professional challenge but which costs you more money for more of his/her time.

**What information must be kept?**

As a minimum you must keep records of the following:

i) All the invoices raised (or rendered) on behalf of the business, either when the goods are delivered or the services supplied, or shortly afterwards. An invoice is a legal document and constitutes a formal demand for money. It must provide enough information to identify the business which sent it, who it was sent to, what it is for and whether VAT is payable.

ii) A list of your Sales invoices numbered sequentially.

iii) All Purchase invoices received, and listed i.e. those demands made on your business for the payment of money.

iv) Wages and salaries paid, and to whom; Income tax and NI contributions paid over to the Tax authorities.
v) All chequebook stubs, paying-in slips/books, counterfoils of petty cash vouchers, business bank account statements. Without these you cannot compile your books of account.
vi) A full record of VAT, whether paid by or paid to the business.

**The advantages of a bookkeeping system for your business**

a) To provide accurate information sufficient to assess whether you are managing the business at a profit or a loss, or whether the business is solvent i.e. is there enough cash available in the business to pay all the outstanding liabilities on demand? The right information of the right kind at the right time is a vital management tool. Good management means making informed decisions of the right kind at the right time based on information that is true and therefore trustworthy.

b) To provide the information required for correct assessments of VAT and Income Tax, so as to avoid financial penalties (and possibly a suspect reputation) for incorrect and/or late payments. HM Customs & Excise keep records for seven years and the Inland Revenue keep them for three years, and so must you. Your accountant will need the best information in order to minimise your tax liabilities, unless of course you decide to submit a statement of income to your Inspector of Taxes without recourse to an accountant. In any event the Inspector will require a calculation of your Income from the business in the form of an Income and Expenditure Account for each trading year.

c) To monitor the behaviour of the business over time by reference to financial summaries "at a glance". You don't need to remember for example how many meals were served in your restaurant business say in this year compared with last year. The comparison that matters is the financial one with reference to the value of those transactions.

**How to record the information you need**
There are basically four methods of bookkeeping. Which one to choose will depend largely on the type and size of business you have established. Take advice from a business adviser or accountant if you are unsure as to which is the best one for your needs.

**a) Proprietary systems.**

These are best suited for sole traders in cash transaction types of business e.g. jobbing builders, market traders or some small shopkeepers. This type of business requires daily record keeping, often including till- rolls for the cash till and offers a simple method of control over finances.

A number of pre-printed stationery systems are available at business bookshops. Select one that allows you enough space to record all that needs recording. Worked examples are set out at the beginning of each book to show you how to keep cash records and the bank position, which can be calculated by following the instructions included. A list of business stationary systems publishers is found at the end of the book.

Cash businesses are more vulnerable than other types for the following reasons: -

i) It is far easier to lose or misplace paperwork. Therefore it is easier to lose control and lose money. Therefore it is more difficult to plan for the future.

ii) It is far more difficult to separate the cash that belongs in the business from the cash belonging to the proprietor.
iii) The Inland Revenue and HM Customs & Excise pay far closer attention to cash businesses because of the greater scope for "creative accounting" and tax evasion.

To minimise these risks, cash business-proprietors are strongly advised to pay their daily cash takings into the bank by using pre-printed paying-in books supplied by their bank. It is also vital to obtain receipts for purchases made from the takings and to keep them in an orderly fashion.

## b) The Analysed Cash book System.

This is perhaps the most common method used by small businesses selling mostly on credit, with perhaps some cash sales. It relies on the Single Entry system of book-keeping, where each entry is, as the name implies, made once only, and all entries are made in one book, the Cash book. The analysed cash book is the "bible" of the business. It allows "at a glance" analysis because it is arranged on a columnar basis, showing how much has been received into the business, when and from where, how much of each receipt is attributable to VAT and therefore how much is the net amount belonging to the business. All this information is written up on one side of a pre-printed book, the left-hand page, showing all monies paid into the bank on behalf of the business. On the opposite, right-hand page are set out in separate columns details of what has been spent by the business, in other words, monies paid out of the bank, to whom and when.

This system is explained and illustrated in greater detail later in this chapter.

## c) The Double Entry System

This method of recording accounts relies on ledgers, or separate books of account for each type of transaction. Far greater detail and control are possible using this system. As well as a cash account there is scope for setting up other ledgers such as the bought ledger for purchases, sales ledger, nominal (or business expense) ledger, salaries and so on.

It is much easier to monitor how much has been spent over a period of time on each type of transaction, simply by referring to the particular ledger or account, on each of which a running balance is struck. Every transaction is recorded in the major account called the Cash Account and also in the appropriate subsidiary ledger. In this way the Cash Account acts as a "Control" account for all the separate accounts of the business.

The most important feature of this system is the characterisation of all bookkeeping entries as either a "credit" ("he trusts" i.e." the business owes him") or "debit" ("he owes"). The sophistication of this method lies in the use of two entries for each transaction. For each credit entry in the Cash Account there must be a corresponding debit entry for the same amount in a different account. Likewise for each debit entry in the Cash Account there must be a corresponding credit entry in a different account. The key words are "equal and opposite". That way the greatest possible degree of control is obtained.

### d) Computerised Accounting Systems

A wide variety of off-the-shelf packages are available, which rely on single or double entry methods. It may be tempting to invest in an accounts package at the outset, especially if you intend to use other computer packages in the business. It would be most unwise to start using such a package without understanding the principles that underlie them.

Businesses have failed because of the familiar - "GIGO" - garbage in, garbage out. Money is the lifeblood of the business so don't turn it into garbage by neglecting an understanding of the what, why and how of bookkeeping.

## Raising finance

It is probable that at some time you will need to borrow some money. Lenders have three basic considerations when looking at an application for a loan-the project, the people behind the project and the lending market currently existing.

There are a number of main options open to you for the financing of your business:

- Investment by an individual, either in the form of capital or a loan.

- Institutional investors

- Bank loans and overdrafts

- Grants, loans and assistance from government sources

- Payment from the Enterprise allowance

- Hire purchase or the leasing of plant

- Mortgage or rental of property

- Factoring of debts or invoices

- Loans against endowment policies

89

- Loans from suppliers in specialist industries

Any of the above categories of financing may be suitable for you and your business-more likely a combination of several. You should remember that every business decision has a financial implication and finding the right type of finance for your business could mean the difference between make or break.

It is highly advisable, if you need more detailed advice or assistance concerning finance, that you contact your local business advice centre. These centres are there to assist all potential or existing businesses and will provide someone who is expert in this particular field to advise you.

Now read the key points from Chapter 7

# Key points from Chapter 7

- A profit and loss forecast is a projection of what sales you think you will achieve.

- A cashflow forecast forecasts the changes in the cash which comes into and out of your bank account each month.

- It is vital to understand the principle and practice of over trading.

- You need to keep clear and accurate records at all times.

- You should fully understand the basic principles of bookkeeping.

- There are a number of main options that you will need to consider in relation to raising finance for your business.

# EXAMPLE BUSINESS PLAN

# 8

# YOUR BUSINESS PLAN

The following pages represent the basis for your business plan and the various sections relate to the sections of the book. If there are parts that you do not feel are relevant to your business, then you should ignore them.

You should construct your own business plan using the following as a guide. By referring to the book and also to the details of your own business you should be in a position to formulate your own plan which will be the complete document for your use, particularly for presentation to your bank manager or to other parties. Remember, it has been stressed throughout the book that an impressive business plan goes a long way towards developing your business and raising the necessary funds to go forward.

**Your Business Plan**

**Name of business**

_____

Address_____

_____

Telephone
Number_____

Sole Trader____    Partnership_____    Franchise___

Limited Company_____

Start up date_____

Type of
Business_____

**Planning ahead (see Chapter one)**

My ultimate goal is

_____
_____
_____
_____
_____
_____
_____

**I expect to achieve the following over the next few years**

Year
1_____

_____

Year
2_____

_____

Year
3_____

_____

## Marketing

I have identified my market
as_____

_____

_____

_____

_____

_____

_____

_____

_____

_____

_____

My customers may be described
as_____

_____

_____

_____

_____

_____

_____

_____

_____

_____

_____

_____

## Product comparison table

My  Product                    Competitor  A
Competitor B

---

Price

Quality

Availability

Customers

Staff Skills

Reputation

Advertising

Delivery

Location

Special Offers

After Sales Service

My product is special because

## The main advantages of my product over my competitors are

**Pricing**

Calculating your break even point

Personal Drawings

_____

_____

National Insurance

_____

_____

Tax

_____

_____

Stationary

_____

_____

Advertising

_____

_____

Telephone

_____

_____

Rent and Rates

_____

_____

## Heating and Lighting

Vehicle Depreciation

_____

_____

Petrol

_____

_____

Servicing

_____

_____

Road Tax Fund

_____

_____

Insurance

_____

_____

Business Insurance

_____

_____

Bad Debts

_____

_____

Premises
My business will be located at

_____

_____

_____

_____

_____

Because

_____

_____

_____

_____

_____

_____

Details of my lease/licence/rent/rate/next rent review

_____

_____

_____

_____

_____

Details of key staff (if any

Name_____

_____

Position_____

_____

Address_____

_____Age_____

_____

Qualifications_____

_____

_____

Relevant work experience

_____

_____

_____

_____

_____

_____

Present
Income_____

_____

Repeat as necessary

I will need to buy in the following skills during the first
two years

_____

_____

_____

_____

_____

I estimate the cost of employing people or buying any
services I may need in the first two years

Number of people       Job Function       Monthly Cost
Annual cost_____

My personal Details
Name_____

Address

_____

_____

_____

_____

_____

Telephone
(home)_____

_____

Telephone
(work)_____

_____

Qualifications_____

_____

_____

_____

_____

Date of
Birth_____

_____

Business experience

_____

_____

_____

_____

_____

Courses attended

_____

_____

_____

_____

_____

_____

## Book-keeping

I intend to keep the following records
(which will be kept up to date by myself/book-
keeper/accountant)

_____

_____

Other

Accountant

_____

_____

Address

_____

_____

Telephone_____

_____

Solicitor_____

Address

_____

_____

_____

_____

_____

_____

Telephone_____

VAT Number_____

Insurance
Arrangements_____

Raising finance

By reference to my profit and loss and cashflow
forecast, I need to borrow

Amount £

_____

For

_____

_____

Period

_____

_____

I am investing £

_____

_____

_____

I can offer the following security

_____

_____

_____

## CONCLUSION

The aim of this book is to ensure that, having read and understood all the key stages of business development, that you are now in a position to formulate an effective business plan.

To many people, the very word 'business plan' makes them very nervous because it means work, often delving into areas that are beyond an individuals control. If you go to a bank manager for a loan, he or she will always ask to see a business plan in order to gain the confidence to lend money. Without a business plan, to the bank manager at least, a person is proceeding in an unstructured way, often taking unacceptable risks, and cannot accurately forecast where the business will be in 6 months or one years time.

It is hoped that, having worked your way through the areas of business development and understood the model business plan laid out in chapter seven, that you will find the process of planning that much easier.

A word of advice: if you are in the process of starting up a business, always plan and plot a way forward that will enable you to see the coming year(s) very clearly. This will be of benefit to both yourself and also those who you wish to get on your side in the future, be it a bank manager or government department.

If you are a business in the process of trading and need a plan, put aside time to do this, it is perhaps the most important element in the business process.
Good luck!

## Useful Addresses

Advisory Conciliation and
Arbitration Service (ACAS)
Clifton House
83-117 Euston Road
London NW1 2RB
Tel 0207 369 5100

Association of British
Chambers of Commerce
7 Tufton Street
London SW1P 3QB
Tel 0207 222 1555

Association of Independent
Business
38 Bow Lane
London EC4M 9AY
Tel 0207 329 0219

BNR Business Names Registration
Somerset House
Temple Street
Birmingham B2 5DN
Tel 0207 643 0227

British Franchising Association, Franchise Chamber
Thames View
Newtown Road
Henley on Thames
Oxon RG9 1HG, Tel 01709 578049

British Overseas Trade Board
1-3 Victoria Street
London SW1E 6RB
Tel 0207 215 5000

British Technology Group
101 Newington Causeway
London SE1 6BU
Tel 0207 403 6666

Business in the Community
8 Stratton Street
Mayfair
London W1X 6AH
Tel 0207 629 1600

Business Links
See local phone books or
Small firms and business links
Division

Department of Trade and Industry
Level 2
St Marys House
Sheffield S1 4PQ
Tel 0114 259 7507

The Chartered Institute of
Patent Agents
Staple Inn Buildings
High Holborn
London WC1V 7PZ
Tel 0207 405 9450

Companies Registration Office
Companies House
Crown Way
Cardiff
CF4 3UZ
Tel 01222 388588

Confederation of British
Industry (CBI)
Centrepoint
103 New Oxford Street
London WC1A 1DU
Tel 0207 379 7400

Department of Social Security
Richmond House
79 Whitehall
London SW1A 2NS
Tel 0207 210 5983
Freephone 0800 666 555

Department of Trade and Industry
1-3 Victoria Street
London SW1E 6RB
Tel 0207 215 5000

Department for Education and Employment
Moorfoot
Sheffield S1 4PQ
Tel 0114 275 3275

Forum for Private Business
Ruskin Chambers
Drury Lane

Knutsford
Cheshire WA16 6HA
Tel 01565 634467

Health and Safety Executive
Chancel House
Neasdon Lane
London NW10 2UD
Tel 0208 459 8855

International Association of
Book keepers
Burford House
44 London Road
Sevenoaks
Kent TN13 1AS
Tel 01732 458080

National Federation of
Small Businesses
32 Orchard Road
Lytham St Annes
Lancashire FY8 1NY
Tel 01253 720911

Scottish Enterprise
120 Bothwell Street
Glasgow G2 7JP
Tel 0141 248 2700

Small Business Bureau Ltd
Curzon House
Church Road
Windlesham

Surrey GU20 6BH
Tel 01276 452010

Welsh Development Agency (WDA)
Pearl House
Greyfriars Rd
Cardiff CF1 3XX

English Enquiry 0345 775577
Welsh Enquiry 0345 775566

Easyway Guides

For a full list of books in the Easyway guides series, and in the Straightforward Guide series, please contact us at: 106 Ladysmith Road Brighton BN2 4EG. 01273 695152

www.straightforwardco.co.uk.

For     information     contact     us     at: info@straightforwardco.co.uk.

Notes to the business plan pages 90-98 You should note any useful information or ideas you might have whilst reading this book.

# Notes

# Notes

# Notes

# INDEX